How to Grow Your
Transcription Business

How to Grow Your Transcription Business

◆

in the Technology Turbulence Ahead

Nicholas J. Mahurin

iUniverse, Inc.
New York Lincoln Shanghai

How to Grow Your Transcription Business
in the Technology Turbulence Ahead

iUniverse books may be ordered through booksellers or by contacting:

iUniverse
2021 Pine Lake Road, Suite 100
Lincoln, NE 68512
www.iuniverse.com
1-800-Authors (1-800-288-4677)

Disclaimer: The views expressed in this book are the opinion and observations of the author. While many may read the author's comments as recommendations or suggestions, please do not take any such statements to constitute legal, accounting or consulting advice. While the author is an executive of InfraWare, Inc., even statements regarding InfraWare, its products and services should not form the basis of significant business decisions. All circumstances are unique, conditions change over time, and the views presented in this book are for the reader's consideration of further investigation and judgment.

ISBN: 0-595-34482-8

Printed in the United States of America

This book is dedicated to the ongoing success of the small-and medium-sized transcription service organizations in communities across the U.S. that play a crucial yet unsung role in healthcare and other important aspects of our lives.

Contents

Preface

Skilled, dedicated workers operate small transcription service organizations across the United States. This noble profession is largely invisible to most Americans because this important layer of healthcare operates behind the scenes, in the hidden offices of healthcare facilities, small, discreet office buildings and private homes.

Leaders of these organizations face many challenges: Demand for their service grows, but qualified workers are not readily available for hire. Large organizations have begun using low-cost overseas workforces, and there is an additional, impending tide of change from the improving performance of speech recognition technology.

The fragmented nature of this cottage industry leads it to change slowly, and the modest size of typical companies leaves them without deep resources to apply to information technology, research and development or political action.

This book is vital at this time because it provides the managers of these service companies insight into how to prepare for the evolving market conditions. When many drivers for change converge in an industry, an evolution occurs. Such a step is usually good for the overall economy, but it generates turbulence that can be difficult for existing providers to handle. Fortunately, those who exercise courage in the face of such changes will find an opportunity to leverage their experience and knowledge to achieve even greater success.

My background as an information technology engineer led me to speech recognition and automation technology, but my background as an entrepreneur led me to write this book. Business management is a passion of mine, and I have weathered changing business conditions in my own career. Drawing from this information, I hope to empower managers and business owners with insight and resources to seize opportunity from the turbulence ahead.

Introduction

May you live in interesting times.

—Author Unknown[1]

The landscape in which transcription service organizations operate faces dramatic change in the very near future. Challenges in maintaining enough capacity to meet customer needs, competitive threats posed by offshore competitors and advances in technology will certainly shake up this calm cottage industry of nearly a quarter-million skilled workers.

From the very beginning, this book starts with the premise that the reader owns or manages a transcription service organization. As the owner of a small business or the manager of the medical records or transcription department in a healthcare facility, the reader of this book should:

- believe there is currently strong demand for transcription work which could support growth and service improvements, if only more qualified workers were available for hire, and

- share the concern that, in the long-term, advances in Speech Recognition Technology (SRT) could shake up the traditional transcription business by introducing pricing pressures and reducing dependency on professional workers.

I subscribe to these fundamental assumptions, but I also have a clear vision of an opportunity for a bright future for medical transcription organizations. This book will unfold that vision. These chapters will explore the current state of the industry, compare this industry to others which have already made similar transitions and examine the larger economic forces at work. This book will validate the above assumptions and the impending threats that follow for those who choose to ignore them. Finally, this book will demonstrate the potential to simulta-

---

1. Many people believe this quote to be an ancient Chinese curse. Research shows that to be unlikely, but the quote is fascinating.

neously grow revenues and grow profit margins today while extending the competitive relevance of the business into the future.

As the largest segment of the overall transcription industry, this book focuses on medical transcription. Many of the observations in this book hold true for the broader transcription industry as well.

As the guide through this journey, I hope to help prepare readers for the turbulence ahead. Indeed, periods of change represent as much opportunity as they do risk. We live, and work, in an interesting time.

There is a commercial element to this book. As the CEO of a company that develops innovative solutions for the transcription service industry, the same views that shape my company have shaped my writing. Naturally, pride in my team's work and accomplishments tend to shine through.

Recognizing the challenges in writing, Mark Twain once said, "I didn't have time to write a short letter, so I wrote a long one instead." As a business manager myself, I understand the scarcity of time so I have endeavored to produce a short book to brief the reader quickly.

First, some housekeeping. Take special note of the symbol below. Throughout the book, this symbol indicates that the current topic is further developed on the Web site that complements this book. By going online to the address listed, the reader can garner a more in-depth perspective about each topic.

----

①Internet Expansion
www.infraware.com/growbizbook/

While acronyms can be confusing to readers, they can also be helpful. Both the healthcare and technology fields use acronyms extensively, and they are used throughout this book. Acronyms are expanded at least the first time they are used. They can also be found in a handy glossary in the back of the book.

With that out of the way, let's get started!

PART I
Navigating a Transforming Industry

1

Transcription Industry

The test of a first-rate intelligence is the ability to hold two opposed ideas at the same time, and still retain the ability to function.

—F. Scott Fitzgerald

Business managers already have a valuable perspective on the landscape of the transcription service industry. As soldiers on the ground fighting the daily battles of running a small business[1], they continuously win incremental victories for themselves, their customers and their employees. Occasionally, we all need to break from the daily process of managing our affairs to lift our heads above the trees to take in a broader view.

The microeconomics of business organization and costs per line in this industry are well-known to everyone who is working as a contractor or subcontractor. The macroeconomics of this industry are worth a fresh look as we begin, because it is easy to lose sight of the forest when standing among the trees. In this chapter, we will look at the big picture over time to establish some common ground and lay the foundation for reaching conclusions on which to base a forward-looking strategic plan.

The current state of the industry is perhaps best described as the *calm before the storm*. Every part of the value chain is strained, and innovation is maturing rapidly in the wings. To grasp the full picture, we will take a look at the history of transcription, the development of speech recognition technology (SRT), and finally, the current state of the industry.

Some of this early text might seem a bit dry, but I think it is helpful to establish a baseline of facts upon which we can build more interesting analysis in later

---

1.   In this context, small business means an organization of 1 to 200 people. Even more importantly, the term business is used loosely in this text. It applies to internal departments as well as independent businesses.

chapters. This book is not long, so I challenge you to stick with it. The pace will pick up quickly.

TRANSCRIPTION HISTORY

Written medical records date back to some of the earliest human writings. Some estimates go back as far as 3000 B.C. Many papyri were written in the period of 1000 to 2000 B.C. These early forms of healthcare documentation include many generations of media, including metal plates, clay tablets, stone walls, papyrus, parchment and eventually paper. Today, we are in the midst of yet another change of media as healthcare systems leave elaborate paper filing systems in favor of Electronic Medical Records (EMR, also known as EHR or Electronic Health Records). Many MTs have witnessed this with their customers already.

Of course, computer technology has come to the industry in phases. Manual typewriters were replaced by electronic typewriters and finally by personal computers (PCs) in the 1970s and '80s, respectively. These steps improved productivity and convenience by making it easier to correct errors and to reuse common text (such as *normals*[2]). Communication technology has helped, too. Modems and private phone lines gave way to Internet connections and broadband, which allow the flexible distribution of digital audio dictation files as well as typed reports.

These developments have served small transcription service companies by enabling them to conveniently rely on a distributed work force. Since the changes were introduced incrementally over time, the impact seemed minimal to most workers and their employers. Few, however, could imagine going back to manual typewriters and typing erasers.

CURRENT INDUSTRY STATUS

The current state of this unique industry is as interesting as it is challenging. My work as a consultant and business leader in the industry provides a bird's eye view of conditions and trends. Few people outside the industry have any idea of its significance. Even insiders can lose track of the big picture. InfraWare's[3] market research indicates the following major highlights:

---

2.   Normals are standard blocks of text used by authors in typical circumstances to save time. A radiologist, for example, might dictate, "my normal chest x-ray", which instructs the transcriptionist to insert a predefined paragraph.

- $10-$20 billion (U.S. dollars) in annual revenue, growing at about 10% per year

- 240,000 U.S. transcription workers

- 100,000 self-employed U.S. workers (of the 240,000)

- Demand for 300,000 U.S. workers, representing a 60,000-worker shortfall

- The industry is highly fragmented, with the largest competitor holding less than a 5% share of the overall market

The outlook for the industry is even more interesting. Building an outlook based only on the above facts, one might conclude that this is a wonderful bed of roses in which to work. But there are two primary concerns that I hear from the business owners with whom I consult:

- There is a lack of available, qualified workers that prevents growing the business, even with customer demand; and

- As SRT gets traction with healthcare facilities, a fear surfaces that one's business could become obsolete in the long term.

AAMT

The American Association for Medical Transcription (AAMT) is evidence of this vibrant community of skilled workers. Founded in 1978, this association serves its membership by promoting an understanding of the work of MTs. They also represent the interests of a large field of otherwise non-connected members in legislative and regulatory matters.

Under current leadership, AAMT is growing. At the end of 2004, the organization boasted approximately 8,400 members. Launching a new initiative for legislative influence on behalf of their members, they recently chose to relocate their CEO to Washington, D.C. In January 2005, AAMT added to their successful Journal of the American Association for Medical Transcription (JAAMT) periodical by publishing the inaugural issue of Plexus, a magazine focused completely on helping MTs keep pace with their evolving field.

---

3.   InfraWare, Inc. (InfraWare.com) is the company I manage. We serve the transcription service industry.

MTIA

The Medical Transcription Industry Association (MTIA) is another industry association that serves the needs of medical transcription companies and health information management professionals. With an emphasis on Medical Transcription Service Owners (MTSOs), MTIA holds an annual conference that has become a *must attend* event for many in the industry.

To learn more about industry associations and activities, point your web browser to this address:

ⓘInternet Expansion
www.infraware.com/growbizbook/orgs

CATALYSTS FOR CHANGE

In addition to the supply-and-demand gap, a number of catalysts have come together to promote change in the industry. The Health Insurance Portability and Accountability Act (HIPAA) is one of the most powerful. Privacy policies have traction, and the old practices of storing medical information in non-secured data stores and communicating it over unencrypted network circuits is quickly becoming unacceptable. Modern, secure storage and communication methods are needed across the board. When such changes are implemented, it becomes far more likely that strategic decision-makers will consider changes in peripheral services such as medical transcription as well.

Other catalysts include the adoption of EMR systems and offshoring, or out-sourcing to overseas firms. EMR systems replace old paper records with more elaborate, detailed computer databases. While the medical industry converted to electronic billing systems two decades ago to cope with the complexity of insurance filings and accounts receivable, many healthcare facilities have kept the status quo for patient charts. These systems are steadily being replaced with electronic systems for many reasons—including privacy and improved patient care. EMR systems promote more in-depth interaction between the transcription service provider and the healthcare organization. It is reasonable to believe that hospitals, for example, might begin to require external transcriptionists to post their reports to HL7 database gateways[4] in the near future so that the data do not have to be double-handled.

Offshoring refers to outsourcing work to low-cost overseas workforces. It is primarily associated with information technology services, such as call centers and transcription shops. Recent events, however, show that this trend might slow down for medical transcription. In 2003, a Pakistani transcription subcontractor contacted the University of California San Francisco Medical Center to request payment for her services. She had been hired by the third party responsible for providing service to the healthcare facility. The hospital declined payment with the appropriate explanation that her contractual arrangement was not with them. In response, the transcriptionist e-mailed a copy of a patient's medical file to the hospital with a threat to post that one and many others on a Web site if she was not paid. Naturally, the facility sent payment to avoid the potential damage to their patient and their own reputation, but this case pointed out a very serious risk in using offshore firms. If the service provider had been a U.S. firm, the hospital could have sought a resolution through the law by simply requesting that a judge issue an injunction to prevent her from carrying out the threat. Since this person was outside the U.S., she was not under the jurisdiction of HIPAA or the U.S. courts. This eye-opening experience raised a caution flag for this type of arrangement. The State of California even introduced legislation to protect patients against use of such firms. Due to the risks and loss of control in these circumstances, other solutions are more viable.

For more information about HIPAA and the impact on transcription service businesses, follow this Internet link.

ⓘInternet Expansion
www.infraware.com/growbizbook/hipaa

Offshoring is a political hot-button. Most Americans have strong feelings against outsourcing important service jobs overseas. Two fundamental reasons contribute to the market drifting in that direction. The first is the supply/demand gap in the U.S.: There simply aren't enough qualified domestic workers to produce all the reports. The other significant factor is cost. Under enormous pressure to contain the growth rate of medical service costs, healthcare organizations target

---

4.   HL7 database gateways serve the purpose of distributing healthcare related information among various computer systems in a facility with multiple systems. Health Level 7 (HL7) itself is a protocol used in the communication process.

those that they perceive to be only indirectly related to patient care. Underdeveloped or developing nations have labor costs far below those in the U.S.

Speech recognition technology presents an interesting alternative to offshoring. If SRT can close the supply/demand gap by leveraging the efforts of U.S. workers with intellectual assets, and if it can reduce the overall cost of processing the average line, it has the potential to eliminate the need for offshoring. To an industry insider, this might sound like a choice between two evils, but keep an open mind about SRT as we continue this journey. There is plenty of upside potential for the MT service organization.

2

Change is Inevitable

In the business world, the rearview mirror is always clearer than the windshield.

—Warren Buffett

TECHNOLOGICAL REVOLUTION

In this chapter, we will explore examples of threatening changes in other industries, including two from my own business experience. We will relate the lessons learned to the broader economy and the specific road ahead in the transcription service industry. While all industries have unique characteristics, history shows that they also share some common ground. Following the work of early researchers and pioneers, the proceeding evolution goes through many stages. We can learn a lot from that history which we can apply to our situation.

From inception, all industries evolve. The opportunities and challenges involved in operating a business in a particular industry vary dramatically as changes occur. In fact, such evolutionary changes yield the most significant business challenges and opportunities.

As drivers of small businesses, our success lies in the accuracy of our assumptions about the business conditions to come. When changes occur in our industry or competitive market, it is analogous to a curve in the road. Those who ignore a curve by continuing to drive straight will likely suffer and quite often fail. Those who accurately plan for and navigate the road will benefit from the rewards of more business and higher profit margins.

When we discuss change, consider two categories: Evolutionary change is incremental and includes the year-to-year refinements and developments found in all growing industries. This type of change is missing in only the most mature of industries, which are usually associated with a lack of competitive innovation. Revolutionary change is found early in the lifecycle of an industry or when technology crosses over from another industry. Such is the case for the transcription service industry. Until recently, change has been, for the most part, slow and incremental. While word processing and communications technologies have had significant impacts on the industry, none has fundamentally changed the core method of production or the overall value of the service. SRT has the potential to do both.

CARRIAGES

Prior to the rise of the automobile, horse-drawn carriages were common. Manufacturers of carriages prospered across the U.S. Today, we don't find any such businesses. Most entrepreneurs who once made a good living in this field ended up suffering a slow erosion of their business as the automobile revolution unfolded. There is one notable exception.

William C. "Billy" Durant of Flint Michigan successfully built carriages in the late 1800s. As the end of the 19th century approached, Durant and other carriage builders held the young automobile industry in contempt. From their perspective, the new technology had many shortcomings. It also threatened the industry in which they earned their livelihood. In a moment of insight, Durant recognized the impressive performance of a Buick automobile. In that moment, he set aside the bias from his past to see his modern competition again, as if for the first time. Soon afterward, Durant joined Buick and went on to run the company. Later, he formed General Motors (GM), using Buick as a base. GM, of course, went on to become the world's largest automaker.

EVOLUTION OF THE PC INDUSTRY

The PC industry offers an interesting example of a quickly maturing industry. When IBM introduced its PC in 1981, the company used off-the-shelf components and chose not to protect the architecture (as Apple Computer had) from "clone" builders. Compaq[1] Computer Corp released their own compatible PC immediately after IBM's release. By the late '80s, more than one hundred PC builders advertised. In communities across the U.S., a mammoth industry had been born. There were few barriers to entry, and many entrepreneurs staked a claim.

---

1.   Compaq actually stands for "Compatibility and Quality".

In 1989, only 6 months after earning my engineering degree from Rose-Hulman Institute of Technology, I staked my own claim in the PC business. With a startup company called Computer Solutions (CS), I began building and selling personal computers that were essentially clones of IBM PCs. At the time, we could offer customized computers built to order at less that half the cost of an IBM or Compaq machine. In just a few short years, we had achieved significant market share in our own community and had grown to another, larger market. We installed several generations of computers in law firms, college campuses, manufacturing plants, healthcare facilities and more. CS reached $1 million in annual sales in less than two years. In addition to hardware, we became very proficient in the services needed to deploy computers in local area networks (LANs) to accomplish our customers' goals. At the time, we still considered ourselves a *products* company, but we prided ourselves in the quality of our services. Customer satisfaction with the total solution kept them coming back for more year after year.

By our fifth year, we had begun to realize how important networking and other professional services had become to the business. The services had become a profit center. They accounted for only 20% of gross revenue, but they yielded much better profit margins. More importantly, we thought, the services drove hardware sales and fostered customer loyalty.

Next, the unthinkable happened. The pricing gap between CS Systems and top-tier, national-brand computers narrowed. Before we knew it, Compaq and IBM offered computers on retail shelves at prices competitive to our own. Only a year or so later, prices became so competitive that they caused us to reduce our margins to stay comparably priced. A dark period followed in which both revenues and margins declined slowly over a several-year period beginning in 1995. While we stayed the same, those external market factors drove our profitable, growing business into a shrinking business that was posting losses.

If we had remained rigid, the business would have failed. Fortunately, we did not. We asked ourselves the right questions, including:

- *Why do our loyal customers use us?*

- *What do they like best about us?*

- *Why have some customers left us?*

At first, we answered with the shallow messages we had been spawning for years. *Our own press*, you might say. As we kept working on the problem, we eventually uncovered the valuable truth: While most of our revenues were for hardware, most of our profit was earned by services. The support services we had built to facilitate computer sales had become what our customers valued most. It took a lot of courage to change the focus of the business. We even had to set aside some pride, but we did it. We discontinued the production of computers and focused on services. Gross revenue declined, but margins and customer satisfaction improved. This new focus allowed us to improve our service even further. Eventually, we were posting profits and growing again. Just as importantly, we had found a niche that was more sustainable.

Ten years after that crisis began, CS is still in business and is as successful as ever. 2004 gross revenues were 60% less than they had been 10 years prior, but net profit at the bottom line was even higher than it had been in that heyday year. Customers are loyal, the staff is mature and the outlook is bright. In this same 10-year period, more than 70% of PC builders have gone out of business. They failed to adapt and went down with their ships.

This example of a changing industry demonstrates the brutal reality of our free-market system. In the big economic picture, it is healthy. For the entrepreneur trying to navigate a business, such a change can seem arbitrary. It can be torture and rarely has a happy ending.

I wish there had been a roadmap to navigating the change that we needed without the painful learning experiences, lost profits and risks we had to take. As the medical transcription industry begins to change, many (probably most) owners of these businesses will respond too late or too little to save their businesses. Others will show courage and clarity of vision by driving change to their own benefit, taking advantage of this shift in technology.

One of the greatest strengths of a small business is the ability to adapt quickly to new conditions, and to take advantage of anticipated developments in market conditions when it's economically feasible to do so.

EVOLUTION OF THE INTERNET SERVICE INDUSTRY

Today, nearly everyone in mainstream America has an Internet connection. Many of us have broadband at home and at work. In the early to mid-'90s, however, this eventual development was anything but obvious.

Although the Internet had existed in some form for decades, the proliferation of personal computers and the development of the World Wide Web[2] (WWW) in 1994 brought it out of the academic arena and into the private sector, to the masses.

It was high-risk entrepreneurial pioneers who first brought the Web to private businesses and homes. Cable companies, telephone companies and big businesses couldn't have been further away from the discussion. At the time, private citizens and businesses were online, but only in private venues such as CompuServe, Prodigy and AOL, none of which was a part of the Internet yet. (At the time, these companies had private, non-connected online communities to which users could connect to share information.)

The business opportunity was for those small-business entrepreneurs who had the vision of what the Internet would become. Those pioneers, mostly sole proprietors and small businesses, took a great deal of risk by installing T1s, modems and phone lines to bring the Internet experience to their community via a local telephone number. Those risks paid off, and most were successful. End of story? Hardly!

As the number of subscribers to these small Internet service providers (ISPs) grew, the business model got the attention of others who had been watching from the sidelines. AOL, for example, competed with the Internet experience. While many people consider AOL to be almost synonymous with the Internet today, they were originally a private service that did not anticipate the overwhelming growth of the Web. The company competed effectively with the more established online providers in the early to mid-'90s by providing rich content and an easier-to-use interface. Still, by the mid-'90s, the trend continued in favor of the Internet.

One of the first major shifts in this industry was by those incumbent online providers. Despite their best efforts to hold their subscribers' attention, the momentum of the Internet couldn't be ignored. In an about-face, AOL and others attached their networks to the Internet. Instead of continuing to compete with the Internet and risk becoming obsolete, they joined the rampage to the Web, and used it to their advantage. Of course, AOL went on to become the world's largest ISP. Imagine how wise a move that turned out to be. And imagine how it looked to the small, family-owned ISPs around the country. It must have seemed frustrating, even unfair.

The next phase was far worse for the small ISP owner. Telephone companies were making lots of money from ISPs. There arose a whole new industry that

---

2.   The Web consisted of the development of the protocols that created the Web server and the Web browser, which is the *face* of the Internet to which most of us relate.

relied on new telephone lines for modem connections. ISPs were surprised to see the telephone companies themselves launch competitive Internet service offerings. After all, the telephone company was their vendor and partner. Business scholars call this "channel conflict." Business owners call it getting kicked around by a big-business monopoly.

Next, cable companies entered the picture with low-cost broadband solutions. This was good for the consumer, but most cable companies wouldn't allow local ISPs to use the cable network to deliver service—so they had to stay in the telephone company camp. Soon, the telephone companies offered DSL, which allowed small ISPs to provide broadband, but the phone companies offered it directly to consumers, too. Within two to three years, the phone companies were offering DSL circuits to the public at even lower costs than they offered to ISPs on a wholesale basis. If that wasn't enough to rattle the small-business ISPs, price wars among the big cable and telephone companies followed. As the big guys battled it out on television, with promotions for free service, the pioneers who had launched the industry could only look on in amazement.

As a computer builder and provider of networking services, I had a keen interest in the Internet once the Web was invented. Since computer-related companies were among the first to use Web sites, it helped my company relate to our vendors to solve problems almost immediately. As a network itself, the Internet was impressive to us, and we saw the possibilities in eventually connecting the closed e-mail systems we had been installing for clients to a global exchange so that messages could cross corporate and geographic boundaries. I considered entry into the ISP business several times before I finally took the plunge in 1998. In retrospect, I wish I had acted more decisively. The opportunity was clear in '96 and '97, but I waited for a sure thing. I waited until the masses were running to the service. It turned out that I wasn't too late to take advantage of the opportunity, but my returns would not be as great as they were for those who had entered earlier.

My own experience in the ISP business was called XSNet (read excess-net). We took our first steps by offering dedicated circuits to business clients in 1997. In mid-'98, having found some success, we spun that off into a full-service ISP, and XSNet was born. Following two years of start-up losses, we operated the company at a profit until I sold it to a regional competitor in 2004 for a handsome profit.

In that short six-to seven-year period of operation, several phases of dramatic change occurred. I experienced firsthand the steady stream of industry shakeups and competitive threats to our business. At some point, growth (as the masses sought out their first Internet connection) gave way to competition for customers who were switching providers. Then we competed by trying to provide unique solutions, and eventually pricing wars developed as sales flattened out over the years leading up to 2003.

As with the PC business, my management team and I studied the circumstances. Unlike the opportunities for change we uncovered for CS, we concluded that the ISP business was maturing at such a pace that our best option was to plan an exit on our own, favorable terms.

We initiated discussions with larger, competitive ISPs that were in a position to purchase our recurring revenue accounts. It took nearly two years to complete a sale from the time we opened those negotiations, but the company was more profitable than ever during that period. Planning for a sale, we held back on new investments with medium-or long-term paybacks. From new servers to advertising, we trimmed costs and rode it out. The company generated significant excess cash flow during that period, and the sale itself provided a very favorable exit.

The point is that in each of these company experiences, factors external to our operation threatened our ongoing business. A decision to continue operating in the same way would have been disastrous, but we learned from our experiences. Each industry and company circumstance is different, but I have learned that it is important not to let such developments catch me off guard. Rather, a successful entrepreneur will recognize the changing environment, take the driver's seat and choose his or her own destiny.

While this overview of trials and tribulations might sound a little depressing, it is actually very healthy. As business owners, we can never afford to lose site of the fact that we're entrepreneurs first, and service providers second. If our business fails, the rest won't matter. Facing these free-enterprise challenges head-on is the only way.

In fact, if not for change in the marketplace, there would be very little opportunity for entrepreneurs to start and grow companies. Large, bulky corporations do well at fine-tuning jobs on a massive scale. Our role is to provide responsive services that escape the giants.

The lesson? Change comes. Those who ignore change pay a high price, but those who see change as an opportunity can take advantage of shifting conditions to grow their businesses and expand their successes. The sooner an entrepreneur identifies a changing marketplace and takes action, the deeper the rewards will be.

It's choice—not chance—that determines your destiny.

—Jean Nidetch

Change is inevitable, and the opportunity to identify changes in the transcription industry is at hand. Fortunately, there is still an opportunity to seize the moment by preparing for the next generation of success. The right actions now will not only avoid obsolescence, but will allow for expansion. After all, someone will have to help the customers of those organizations who keep their heads in the sand until it is too late.

3

Speech Technology Background

I am returning this otherwise good typing paper to you because someone has printed gibberish all over it and put your name at the top.

—An English professor, Ohio University

Accuracy is paramount in this industry. It is a cornerstone of every transcription service business. To continue our study of the market, we need to face the impact of speech recognition head-on. We'll start at the beginning and progress to the present. Don't worry. We'll come back to accuracy.

SPEECH AUTOMATION HISTORY

Research into the concepts of speech technology began as early as 1936 at Bell Labs. In 1939, Bell Labs demonstrated a speech synthesis machine (which simulates talking) at the World Fair in New York. Bell Labs later abandoned efforts to develop speech-simulated listening and recognition, based on an incorrect conclusion that artificial intelligence would ultimately be necessary for success.

In the early 1970s, Lenny Baum of Princeton University invented a mathematical approach to recognizing speech called Hidden Markov Modeling (HMM). The HMM pattern-matching strategy was eventually adopted by each of the major companies pursuing the commercialization of SRT.

The U.S. Department of Defense sponsored many practical research projects during the '70s that involved several contractors, including IBM, Dragon, AT&T, Philips and others. Progress was slow in those early years. It wasn't until the 1980s that SRT was finally commercialized, thanks to continued development and expanding computer processing power. The rapid growth of the evolving personal computer (PC) platform provided a large market with adequate computer power by the late '80s. Still, the software required users to speak in discrete utterances with pauses between words. In the mid-'90s, several companies

17

released more powerful versions that eliminated that limitation. So-called "continuous speech recognition systems" were capable of recognizing natural speech at accuracy levels above 90% under ideal conditions.

Early attempts to apply SRT technology in business settings followed. Many such experiences met with academic success because they *worked*—but simultaneously with disappointment because they didn't work well enough for business-level predictability. Since that time, SRT has experienced many successes and many failures. One of the most fundamental problems came when companies tried to commercialize SRT to large organizations like hospitals. In order to demonstrate a favorable return-on-investment (ROI), they claimed that their SRT systems could eliminate all or most of transcription personnel or outsourcing costs. That simply didn't prove to be the case. Nearly everyone involved in these early approaches experienced disappointment. The failures were represented by a significant gap between the expectations set by the promotional claims and the real-world results. Over time, that gap will shrink. As we look ahead, one thing is sure: SRT has some legitimate strengths, and they are growing. More importantly, for our study of the industry, a new set of expectations might be the key to finally realizing the potential.

LIMITATIONS OF SRT

Let's take a moment to explore the implications of SRT—how it will and how it won't affect the industry, and in particular, the medical transcriptionist (MT). First, what it will not do: In this author's opinion, SRT will impact the nature of the work required of MTs, but it will not eliminate the need for qualified MTs in the foreseeable future. While the programs are efficient and have a lot to offer, they still only achieve accuracy rates in the 90%-96% range at the high end. Those additional few percentage points will be very difficult to achieve. From this level, each incremental fraction of a percentage point gain in accuracy will require an escalating degree of effort. To be trusted, machines will be expected to reliably produce at even higher accuracy levels than the standards set for people. Many people think that such accuracy will not be achievable until there is a breakthrough in the underlying mathematics. To be sure, medical records are far too important to be unchecked or laced with errors.

That said, SRT can still have a dramatic impact on transcription processing *right now*. Properly applied, that impact can be a positive force that helps the MT community, eliminates the underlying need for widespread offshoring and improves the service delivered to healthcare facilities.

The key to unlocking this potential is a shift in perspective. SRT needs to be used by the transcription service organization for its own benefit. The remaining chapters of Part I explore specific methodologies for achieving this success.

4

The Idea is Born

Some people change when they see the light, others when they feel the heat.

—Caroline Schoeder

Traditionally, most people in the medical transcription business get started by serving as transcriptionists. As an information technology entrepreneur, I became interested in the field of transcription as an outsider, from the perspective of technology. My consulting experiences had trained me to identify opportunities in which to apply technology effectively for a wide range of business environments. As a business owner myself, I found it easy to relate to the owners and managers of other small-and medium-sized businesses. My work was nearly always business-driven. That is, I would use technology to solve a business problem that a client presented. The focus was the business challenge, and the technology was a means to an end: utility.

Rarely, but on occasion, I find a technology that is powerful enough that its inherent value is obvious. It actually deserves the search for a business problem. SRT became such a technology for me.

GETTING STARTED WITH TRANSCRIPTION

As I attended Comdex, Networld and other annual IT conventions through the '90s, I enjoyed being exposed to a wide range of trends and innovations. In the context of such large venues (that may include more than 1,000 exhibitors), the key to a successful trip was to ignore most of the booths so I could focus on the opportunities that had ready application for client needs.

Early in the '90s, I found SRT to be curiously interesting. Despite vendor claims, it wasn't ready for mainstream business applications, but it was still interesting that it could work as well as it did. After a five-minute demo at the Dragon or IBM vendor booth, I would move on to more realistic stops. Years later (mid-

'90s), when *continuous speech recognition*[1] arrived, I began to see its business potential more clearly. Still, it had shortcomings and didn't match the needs of my firm's client base.

As the years passed, I noted the steady improvements in SRT performance. I also noticed that despite the cumulative progress, the rate of adoption of the technology remained fairly low at the turn of the 21st century. Finally, I began an informal study of the status of the SRT industry with the objective of better understanding the reasons that it had been only lightly adopted by physicians, attorneys and others who dictate routinely in their professions and would therefore have the most to gain.

The findings surprised me, so much so that I hired an MBA (a person with a master's degree in business administration) to research the facts even further. We concluded that the companies promoting SRT software solutions had made several fundamental errors in addressing the market.

Our first observations were general regarding the usability of the technology as it was available, and not specifically related to transcription applications. We noted that nearly all programs attempted to perform the recognition user's speech in real time, as they spoke and watched the screen. Even with very powerful computers, this user experience was frustrating because there was often a delay in with the words appearing on the screen. The combination of this delay with occasional errors in recognition is too distracting for most people to carry on forward-thinking. In other words, the user interface actually hampered dictation.

Of the SRT products which had been most aggressively marketed, we noted many glaring weaknesses. These included:

- Confusion by the delay of real-time words appearing on screen

- End-user avoidance of the complexity of software setup and use

- The unwillingness of professionals to change their work style and habits

- High cost of acquisition and installation

- MOST SIGNIFICANTLY—Professionals generally like the way they currently work, and they resist change—especially if that change involves more work for them.

---

1. *Continuous speech recognition* refers to the advancement that allowed for continuous speech. Early technology required authors to pause with short breaks between words.

Our observations led us to the realization that the existing products were reaching too far and assuming too much about their users and the accuracy of the systems. We could see a clearer path to unlocking the potential to benefit those who needed the help the most.

The first observation was that physicians and other professional dictation authors prefer the existing workflow. That is, they like to be able to dictate easily without the obligation of monitoring the accuracy of a software program and the associated responsibility of making their own corrections. From their perspective, this status was nearly ideal.

Perhaps the most important observation was the recognition of the inherent value of the MT in the accuracy of finished reports. While SRT could consistently achieve accuracy levels in the range of 85% to 95%, that still leaves significant work. Indeed, even 99% accuracy would be inadequate for my family's healthcare. I suspect others feel the same.

As a consequence, SRT can be most valuable when an MT receives the output. Likewise, MTs can actually benefit MORE from the technology than the authors themselves.

At this point in the analysis, we could speculate on a number of opportunities for improvement over the established paradigm. First was the experience of the author's dictation. Clearly, there was a strong resistance to change on their part. Authors had spoken with their actions through the marketplace: only light adoption of the technology despite claims of high return on investment (ROI) from vendors.

The question became, "How can we introduce the technology in a more palatable way to all the parties involved in the workflow?" The solution was as simple as it was elegant: Change as little as possible by interjecting the technology downstream from the author, into the existing flow of work. This dramatic shift in thinking recognized a completely different value proposition. Instead of assuming that authors and their organizations would benefit the most from the service, we observed that the transcription service professionals actually stood to gain more.

The diversity of transcription service organizations complicated that idea. Some are nestled internal to a facility while others are independent service companies to which facilities outsource work. In both cases, the workforce can be broadly distributed geographically with at-home workers and subcontractors. This led to a problem with IT sophistication. Hospitals, large law firms and other end-user organizations possessed a depth of IT personnel to deploy and maintain a system as we envisioned. Small, independent companies representing a significant part of the supply chain, however, did not. How could we develop our vision into a readily adoptable solution for the entire market that needed the benefits?

SOFTWARE AS A SERVICE (SaaS)

In the early days of the Internet, most people became familiar with an ISP. The Internet Service Provider played an important role in bringing the Internet experience to end-users in a form they could adopt. In the late '90s, many ISPs morphed into Application Service Providers (ASPs). Many other ASPs launched from scratch. ASPs provided dynamic content that end-users wanted. Companies like Amazon, Yahoo, Google, Monster and thousands of others built elaborate Web sites that provided an interactive experience customized to the user's need. In essence, rather than providing static documents, they provided a software application experience. As this field matured through the turn of the 21st century, the ASP business model stretched into something often called Software as a Service (SaaS).

SaaS presents a number of benefits for the software publisher and even more for the end users. Publishers enjoy the luxury of developing their applications to run on a fixed server platform in their own data center. This controlled environment is easier to support than preparing an application to run on diverse platforms that might be in use or preferred by end users at their own sites.

Users of the software enjoy the converse position of avoiding the investment, complexity and support of a server application. They can enjoy the benefits of reliable systems yielding high up-time and availability without the costs or headaches involved.

Another important advantage of SasS is the pay-as-you-go opportunity. Instead of making a huge capital investment in the hardware, software and services required to deploy the solution, users can often subscribe to the application service with a reasonable monthly fee. This eliminates risk and keeps the decision process simple. It also means they can begin profiting from the service immediately (assuming the benefits outweigh the subscription fee, which would be the only reason to subscribe) rather than waiting for the payback period of a capital investment to lapse.

The benefits to the user of SaaS solutions continue as they avoid the hassles and costs associated with supporting and upgrading the server-side hardware and software into the future. The marvel of the Internet has made it possible for the software publisher to deliver the benefits of their software while retaining most of the complexity.

The savvy reader will have guessed by now that the InfraWare solution is based on the SaaS model. The benefits of this business model aligned nicely with the challenges of providing the technology to a diverse and geographically distributed community of users which require an easy-to-use service.

5

The Future MT

A problem well stated is a problem half solved.

—Charles F. Kettering

In earlier chapters, we have reviewed the history of the transcription industry as well as that of the technology that is edging into place. We have observed the natural evolution that all industries face at pivotal times. Let's take a look at the ideal scenario for the organization as well as the evolving role of the MT.

IDEAL SCENARIO[1]

Ideally, we would like to provide MTs with the capacity to grow their businesses by producing more lines. We've already established the difficulty in finding qualified workers, so it would be helpful to provide the ability to produce the additional work (lines) with the employees or subcontractors already in place. That will save on supervisory effort and overhead costs anyway. Producing an increased number of lines without additional people would yield a lower cost per line, which not only grows revenues but profit margins as well. (Remember, there is still a significant shortage of qualified workers, so this doesn't place jobs in jeopardy.) Let's go ahead and have reports produced a little faster, too. That will improve turnaround time and improve customer satisfaction. Sound good so far?

What more could we ask? Let's go ahead and ask for insulation from the imminent threat of replacement by SRT. Our deepest fear is that our largest client (or the boss, if we are working inside a facility) will call to explain that the IT department has decided to make an investment in a speech recognition system

---

1.   This ideal scenario is admittedly very simplified for the purpose of making some high level points. While day-to-day business is more complex, this scenario is still useful and valid for our purposes.

that will render our services unnecessary. Short of that call, our next-deepest concern would be for them to approach us with pricing pressure. "Unless we can lower the costs," the call could go, "we will have to consider a technology-based system." Naturally, transcription service organizations need to mobilize to avoid these possibilities.

How in the world could we shield ourselves from these threats? Is it absurd? Too much to ask? I suggest not. In fact, I submit that the fundamental parameters of this ideal scenario are achievable today. Further, I suggest that the business owners who lead the charge by taking proactive steps to implement the solution will realize a much better upside potential than those who wait for the mainstream. The stubborn members of the industry who refuse to change by holding onto practices that worked in the past will suffer, just as countless counterparts from other industries and other periods of time have suffered prior to losing their businesses.

What would be the cost of such a solution? (At this point, I know I would be concerned about getting set up for a high-ticket investment.) Let's go ahead and append to our ideal scenario that we would like to accomplish all of this without a substantial cash investment.

At the time of this writing, this has been my impression of an ideal situation for an MT business moving forward. Times change, and I didn't interview every business owner in the industry—I would like feedback and the perspective from the workers, business owners and managers in the MT industry. Please go to the Internet link below to pass along thoughts, perspectives and ideal scenarios.

Ⓘ Internet Expansion
www.infraware.com/growbizbook/idealscenario

THE FUTURE MT

The scenario we have outlined might be optimal from a management or owner perspective, but what about the medical transcriptionists, those who work in the trenches every day, those upon whose backs the organization rests day in and day out? Well, to stay in the game, they will have to adapt.

This isn't all bad! In fact, it is rather good. History reminds us that machines and automation have made people's lives easier. Today, for example, the job of a farmer is much safer and more comfortable than it was 100 years ago. Imagine if every farmer used oxen to plow their fields. One day, a farmer begins using a tractor. Once this happens, every other farmer would realize that in order to remain competitive, they would have to either buy new equipment or sell their land to the farmer who did buy the new, highly efficient equipment. While the initial transition might be difficult, the benefits would be compelling. The work of farming would improve as those who invested in tractors would enjoy more reasonable working conditions and better earnings. The cost of food to consumers would likely decline. The risk, of course, is to those who continue to try to remain competitive with their oxen.

As cranking out lines through rapid, accurate typing becomes more the work of a machine and less of the MT, the MT actually has some exciting new challenges to embrace. They can become information professionals. In fact, during a recent conversation with Lea Sims, Director of Publications and Communications with AAMT, she used the term Medical Information Technologist to describe her view of the "future MT."

As technology relieves some of the repetitive labor from the MT, they are still the backbone of the quality and accuracy of the medical record. And, as medical records become far more interesting during the same period of transition, it is natural to view the role of the MT as becoming more knowledge-oriented as it becomes less task-oriented. Use of sophisticated software, databases and other information technology components offer the MT the potential for an even more rewarding work experience.

Figure 1, below, demonstrates the convergence at work in the speech recognition and transcription service industries over time. SRT has strong roots in science and theory, as represented by the left vertical edge of the diagram. On the other hand, transcription service is a very practical field, *what works*, represented along the right vertical edge. Over time, SRT has been improving and becoming more practical. Likewise, over the years, transcription service has been becoming slightly more automated. The present time is indicated by the overall labeled Convergence. Moving forward from this point, they will no longer be separate. The value of the two areas converged is much greater than the value of the sum of the parts. In other words, those who use the converged solutions will benefit from the greater tool. Those who try to stay with the old paradigm, on either side, will find themselves at a competitive disadvantage.

InfraWare helps our clients with the process of *selling* these concepts to their MT personnel as well as customer facilities. We recognize that even after a business leader adopts our vision, they still have a job to do in communicating these concepts to stakeholders in their businesses.

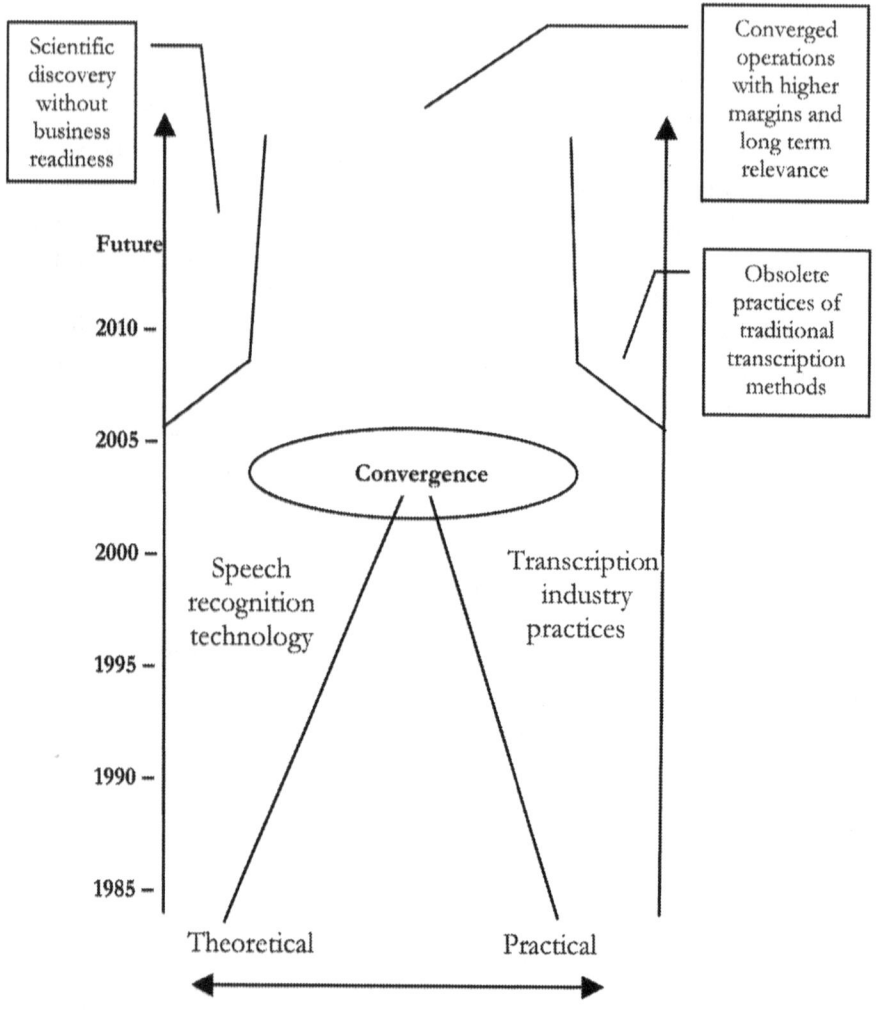

Figure 1 Convergence of the science of speech with the practical nature of transcription.

6

Sketching the Solution

Everything that can be invented has been invented.

—Charles H. Duell, Commissioner,
U.S. Patent Office, 1899

Let's examine the solution from start to finish. Some of this chapter might sound a little self-serving because my colleagues and I formed InfraWare around the same observations upon which I based this text. Naturally, we built our solution around the objectives discussed. I'll just concede upfront that there is a commercial element to this chapter.

To appreciate the solution, it will help to set aside any existing perceptions of speech recognition technology. Keep an open mind. I think any concerns that may be surfacing will be addressed by the time we finish. Try to look at the technology from an opportunistic perspective, rather than a threatening one. We're talking about using SRT to the MT's advantage. The infamous quote by Mr. Charles Duell is one of my favorites. It demonstrates how even intelligent, capable people can be blinded by ignorance and completely miss the power of innovation.

Through the preceding chapters, we have formed a variety of impressions. This chapter will pull together the implications to demonstrate a solution that offers the potential to seize opportunity from the evolving industry conditions.

CAPACITY

Let's say that a certain number of people can accomplish a certain volume of work over a certain period of time. We will call this *capacity*. Managers usually have a good handle on a metric (such as lines per day) for the capacity of their business at any given time. Knowing approximately how many lines personnel can process each day as well as the impact of vacations or other reductions in personnel hours is vital to the business metric. One of the problems with operating a transcription organization is the difficulty in growing capacity to serve more customers or maybe even to keep up with the growth in the amount of work from current customers.

Naturally, we have come to think of capacity as a function of the number of qualified workers we employ. Another possibility is to increase the volume of work that each employee can produce in a given period of time. It goes without saying that productivity varies from worker to worker, but what if we could increase the throughput of each worker by 50 percent, 100 percent, 200 percent or even 300 percent? That might sound unlikely, but the InfraWare implementation of SRT does make such improvements possible. In fact, with only minor adaptation, it can accomplish everything outlined in our ideal scenario.

Of course, the ability to produce these results depends entirely upon the ability to correct documents much faster than they could be typed from scratch. That starts with reasonably accurate First Drafts[1]. A draft with 60 percent accuracy, for example, would probably require more time to correct than to simply be retyped. Once the recognition accuracy rate reaches a range in the 80-or 90-percent range, the process becomes achievable. The challenge then becomes a matter of providing the right productivity software tools to focus on effective correction.

Qualifications of workers become an interesting related subject. Today, the skills required to survive in the MT service field are fairly rigid. I, for example, probably couldn't make a fair living with my 20-words-per-minute typing rate. (We won't even get into accuracy!) How many potential workers have the proofreading skills and the capacity to learn the dictation but will never become fast typists? These people are excluded from the MT ranks today, but they need not be in a future that relies heavily on accuracy in reading and correction and far less on raw typing speed.

PRODUCTION SYSTEMS

The workflow of traditional medical transcription can take on a variety of forms to accommodate various system platforms, but they go something like Figure 2. An author dictates his or her report into a telephone or recorder of some sort. An audio file is captured and queued on a dictation system of some kind (Lanier, Dictaphone, etc.) MTs retrieve jobs from the queue one at a time, and they type

---

1.   The InfraWare platform calls the speech recognition output that is sent to the MT, First Draft.

them at the rate that they are able. Upon completion and approval, the report is finally saved in the patient's medical record. (I simplified the process a bit because systems vary.)

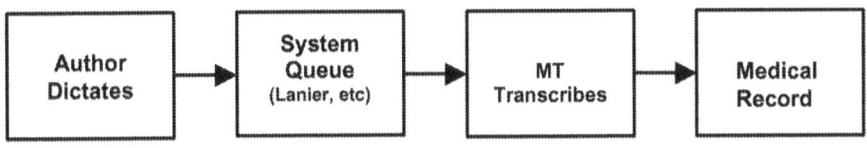

Figure 2

The InfraWare model (Figure 3) makes only subtle changes to the workflow but significant changes to productivity. First, and most importantly, the author's work doesn't change much at all. Physicians find this important. They lack interest in performing any of this work for themselves. In general, they find satisfaction with the status quo in most facilities and are likely to resist dramatic change.

In the new model, the author's dictations get saved to the InfraWare queue. (This is the ASP model discussed in Chapter 4 and made possible and convenient by low-cost broadband Internet connections that already exist at nearly all healthcare facilities today.)

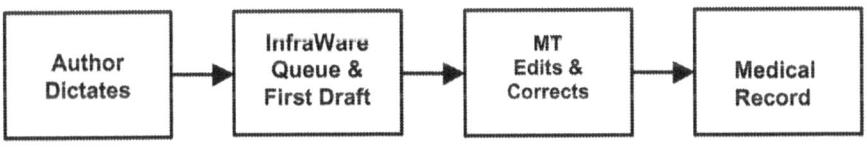

Figure 3

The significance of this is twofold. First, the traditional Lanier-or Dictaphone-style system becomes unnecessary. Second, the dictation becomes available for back-end speech recognition on the InfraWare servers.

Back-end processing solves many of the problems commonly associated with SRT. It eliminates the need for the author to change his or her work habits or interact with speech recognition software, and it isolates any issues presented by imperfect recognition by sending the result directly to the MT, who can ensure the quality of the finished product.

The document generated by the servers certainly isn't perfect. (They are commonly in the range of 85% to 95% accurate.) But the output is valuable to the rest of the process. InfraWare calls the SRT-generated reports a *First Draft*.

Next, an MT retrieves a report to correct and edit. In our system, the MT uses a software program called the InfraWare Transcription Client (ITC). This is a simple but powerful Windows application that allows the transcriptionist to select, retrieve and edit reports. The edit functions are built for speed and they maximize the value of the 90% accuracy of the First Draft. For example, the audio dictation and the text of the First Draft are synchronized. When the user moves through the audio file with the pedals, the cursor in the text is automatically repositioned. Likewise, when the MT moves the typing cursor through the document, the audio is immediately fast-forwarded or rewound to that point.

The primary benefit of using the InfraWare platform is time and productivity. A typical MT can accomplish between two and three times more work each day with the InfraWare system. The cost of using the platform is low, which means both the margins and the volume of work can increase simultaneously. The next chapter deals with margins and the value proposition in more detail.

Additional benefits include greater flexibility for the users at all points in the system as well as with output options as they relate to evolving medical records systems.

INPUT, OUTPUT and VALUE-ADDED PROCESSING

The InfraWare transcription service platform is a very narrowly focused solution. It has the sole purpose of hosting dictation for more efficient transcription processing leveraging technology. Starting within that narrow context, InfraWare works continuously to expand the scope of these aspects of the platform: dictation input, value-added processing and report output.

Input

Fundamental to our platform is the author's desire to use it. In a diverse community of physicians and other authors, we want to provide many methods for capturing dictation. It is important to have a method that is convenient and preferred by each user as well as to provide alternative methods for unique situations. At the time of this writing, the platform currently supports:

> *Telephone*—InfraWare provides a robust telephone dictation system that allows authors to dictate from any land-line telephone via toll-free numbers. The system is user-friendly and feature-rich.

In addition to traditional telephone lines, the system supports Voice-over-Internet-Protocol (VoIP, read "Voice over IP"). VoIP is cutting-edge communication technology that allows telephone calls to be made via broadband Internet lines instead of lines provided by a phone company. In addition to providing modern features, VoIP can also dramatically reduce the cost of operating a system.

Telephone lines can be as costly as $50 per month in commercial settings[2]. An old-style dictation system with eight voice lines can cost as much as $400 per month, plus long distance charges. Utilizing existing broadband connections, VoIP can virtually eliminate those costs.

VoIP is also simple to use. Once IT professionals install a system, using it is nearly identical to using a regular business telephone. The innovative technology is wrapped up in the underlying systems. There is often no training necessary at all.

PC—Dictation by a microphone connected directly to a personal computer (PC) is supported by the InfraWare Dictation Client (IDC). The IDC is a simple-to-use Windows program that allows the author to identify the patient or topic and begin dictating quickly with a minimum of mouse clicks.

PDR—Personal Digital Recorders (PDRs), such as the Olympus DS-330 and several variations of the Pocket PC, such as the HP/Compaq iPAQ. Benefits of this method include portability. The author can carry the device on their person for convenience. The WAV recordings stored on the PDR are retrieved by the author or his or her support staff with the IDC.

VoIP is a fascinating technology that is gaining traction in business as we speak. To learn more, go to this Internet address:

ⓘInternet Expansion
www.infraware.com/growbizbook/voip

Value-added Processing

In addition to the core speech recognition process, the InfraWare platform supports post-recognition value-added processes. The most common of these is "normals substitution." MTs are familiar with substituting a stock paragraph for a radiologist when he dictates something like "my normal chest x-ray." This is a

---

2.   The cost of telephone lines varies by region because they are negotiated between the local exchange carrier and the regulatory commission with local jurisdiction. Commercial lines are often more expensive that residential lines.

wonderful time-saving tool, and MTs are typically credited for those lines. The InfraWare platform is designed to save time for MTs so they can produce two to three times the number of lines in their work day. The normals substitution feature holds these normals in a database and inserts them automatically after the speech recognition step but before the First Draft is sent to the MT. Other value-added steps are under development. For additional information, or to submit ideas for such processing, follow this Internet Expansion link.

ⓘInternet Expansion
www.infraware.com/growbizbook/valueadded

Output

The destination for finished reports is evolving rapidly. While many healthcare facilities still use paper records, that is changing. A significant number of facilities are already using EMR systems, and by 2015, we expect nearly all healthcare facilities to be using EMR. As such, the method of saving or transmitting a finished report to its destination is changing.

Simple printed or electronic "text" is the most common form of reporting, but even external MTs are increasingly expected to insert the finished product of their work into sophisticated medical records database programs. In the context of the InfraWare system, output is generated in the InfraWare Transcription Client. A significant benefit of that program is the forward-looking ability to submit completed reports in a variety of formats to accommodate the health care facility's information technology objectives.

Health Level 7 (HL7) is a protocol used for communication among healthcare database programs. Large facilities often maintain several applications with overlapping sets of data. A consequence is that new information often needs to be distributed to multiple programs. HL7 is used to automate the distribution of such information. Servers known as HL7 gateways are often employed in hospitals to facilitate that objective. Using a software interface, a medical records worker posts data to one screen, and the gateway automatically distributes the data as defined by established rules. The future MT will need to understand the fundamentals of such systems, but they can be easy to use if well equipped with good software.

While HL7 is healthcare specific, eXtensible Markup Language (XML) is a newer, more general protocol. Many modern HL7 gateways accept XML input which can be leveraged by the InfraWare platform. Transcription work completed with the platform can be conveniently transmitted to HL7 gateways in XML format. MTs certainly don't have to learn to design or even fully understand the mechanics of these systems, but they need to prepare for familiarity with the terms, objectives and use of them. The value of their services can be extended by reaching a bit more deeply into the EMR systems of their customers.

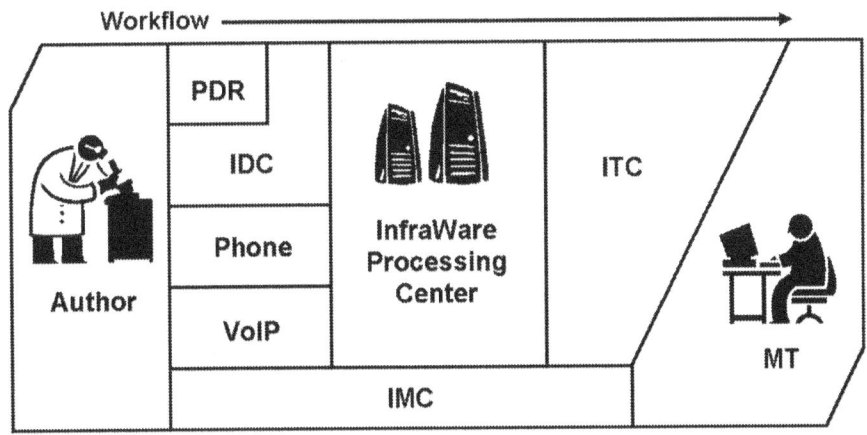

Figure 4

SOFTWARE COMPONENTS

The InfraWare platform uses several powerful software components at the end-user desktop.

InfraWare Dictation Client (IDC)

As mentioned above for input, the IDC is the program that allows an author to dictate directly into a PC. It also supports the connection of a Personal Digital Recorder (PDR) for authors who prefer the mobility offered by these pocket devices.

InfraWare Transcription Client (ITC)

The ITC is a powerful program that runs on the transcriptionist's desktop computer for the purpose of editing and correcting the First Draft to produce a finished report. Designed to be MT friendly, the ITC is designed with features that help accomplish this task in reduced time. As with older programs respected by MTs, the ITC provides the ability to accomplish all tasks from the keyboard (without moving to the mouse) as well as many transcription-specific keystroke shortcuts and a built-in word expander.

InfraWare Management Client (IMC)

The IMC is where *flow* is managed. If the rest of the platform provides the complete transactional experience, the IMC is where a manager runs his or her business. It is a Web-based program which means that it can be run from any location with a secure login. A manager can examine and manage the queue of dictations as well as add, remove and modify user and customer settings.

The purpose of this book is to show you the big picture. If you would like to learn more specifics about the family of InfraWare clients and their respective features, visit this Internet link.

---

①Internet Expansion
www.infraware.com/growbizbook/iwclients

7

Value Proposition

My interest is in the future because I am going to spend the rest of my life there.

—Charles F. Kettering

Let's take a look at the value proposition and how it can change for the better or worse. After all, it *is* changing, and you may spend the rest of your career in a very different future.

MARGINS

Profit margins are the holy grail for small businesses. To help us discuss value, let's define some financial terms. Margin is equivalent to gross profit and can be expressed as either dollars or as a percentage of sales. In Figure 5, for example, the gross profit is $5,250, or 35% (5250 divided by 15,000).

Revenue		
Revenue from Service 1	$10,000	
Revenue from Service 2	$5,000	
Gross Revenue (sales)		$15,000
Cost of Sales		
Wholesale amounts paid to subs, S1	$6,250	
Wholesale amounts paid to subs, S2	$3,500	
Cost of Sales		$9,750
Gross Profit (margin)		$5,250
Expenses		
Rent, utilities	$1,000	
Advertising, payroll, other	$2,500	
Total Expenses		$3,500
Net Profit		$1,750

Figure 5 Defining margin and profit

THE VALUE PROPOSITION

With the help of Figure 6, we can analyze the value proposition of utilizing the InfraWare system as follows:

Start with the top few lines labeled "Current." This represents a typical transcription company at this time without leveraging technology. If a customer pays the business 16 cents per line, and the business pays a contracted employee 10 cents per line, which leaves a gross profit margin of 6 cents per line. Prices and costs vary. Right now, the accuracy of the amounts is not as important as the concept involved. Later, you can perform the same analysis with your own information.

Value Proposition Worksheet

Description	Revenue
Current	
Billing rate to end-user (price)	$.16
Wholesale rate paid to sub (cost)	($.10)
Difference (margin)	$.06
Assume 2-fold productivity increase	
Billing rate to end-user (price)	$.16
InfraWare pre-processing platform cost	($.03)
Wholesale rate paid to sub (cost)	($.05)
Difference (new margin)	$.08
Assume 2.5-fold productivity increase	
Billing rate to end-user (price)	$.16
InfraWare pre-processing cost	($.03)
Wholesale rate paid to sub (cost)	($.04)
Difference (new margin)	$.09
Assume 3-fold productivity increase	
Billing rate to end-user (price)	$.16
InfraWare pre-processing cost	($.02)
Wholesale rate paid to sub (cost)	($.033)
Difference (new margin)	$.107

Figure 6 Note: A blank worksheet is included in Appendix A for working with other data.

Now look at the second section labeled "Assume two-fold productivity increase." This example represents using a system like InfraWare's platform. Notice the price stays the same, but the costs change. In this case, a line has been added for the cost of using the platform. In addition, the subcontractor cost has been reduced by half to 5 cents per line. The result is an 8-cent margin, which is 33% higher than the Current scenario. Why is the subcontractor (or employment) amount reduced to half? It is based on the productivity gain. If there is a two-fold (double) gain in productivity, that means an MT can accomplish twice as many lines in the same time period. In other words, if they were paid half the rate per line, they would make the same amount of money as in the Current scenario. That might sound like a tough message to sell, "Let me cut your rate in half because you will be able to do twice the work." Indeed, it could be. The point of this exercise is to demonstrate the overall savings of the process, which is 2 cents per line[1]. The reality is that the savings is available to share among the transcription service organization, the employee and the customer. Saving 2 cents per line across the entire chain of participants is far better than the alternative of coping with declining margins into the future. What if customers demanded to pay only 15 cents and employees demanded to be paid 11 cents?

The additional sections of Figure E represent the impact of more dramatic productivity improvements. A two and a half productivity increase yields a 9-cent margin which is 3 cents better than Current. Notice that the cost is revised to 4 cents per line (10 cents divided by 2.5). That represents a 50% improvement over Current. The three-fold improvement represents even more dramatic results.

The next logical question becomes. "What improvement in productivity is actually achievable?" Our studies and work with customers demonstrate that improvements greater than two-fold are typical. Several factors contribute to the degree of improvement. It begins with the skill set of the transcriptionist. The top 20% of MTs, for example, have less to gain than the bottom 20%. Since the top performers are already typing fast and accurate, the First Draft might only help them a little[2]. Those MTs in the middle performing range, and especially those in the bottom performing range, have more to gain. They have the potential to

---

1.   At the present time, the actual cost of the InfraWare system is less than 3 cents per line.
2.   It should go without saying that your top 20% of performers are your greatest asset. Any change in compensation planning needs to take their value into consideration and should be presented to them very carefully. Keeping and leveraging their knowledge is crucial, and they should be rewarded for training and mentoring.

reach even a three-fold improvement. (In other words, an MT would produce three times the number of lines per hour of work.)

Strategic managers will want to take advantage of an opportunity to utilize the technology service to maximize the contributions of their slower performers. In fact, many will discover that they can relax their hiring criteria which will open recruiting to a broader field of candidates. Strong work ethic, command of the vocabulary and an eye for accuracy will be as critical as ever, but typing speed itself will be far less important. I, for example, couldn't possibly make a living as a traditional MT. My typing speed is much too slow. My ability to read for accuracy, however, is reasonably strong. Someone with my mix of skills could fair well using the InfraWare platform. This observation opens an entire field of potential workers to your organization.

PART II
Growing a Service Business

8

Entrepreneurship

Two roads diverged in a [yellow] wood, and I—I took the one less traveled by. And that has made all the difference.

—Robert Frost

I had wanted to be an entrepreneur for as long I can remember. I had certainly formed that vision for myself by my teenage years. Like many young people, I had visions of grand success including material wealth, respect and admiration from my peers.

I imagined a career, a lifestyle in fact, that would involve a lot of work. I was right about that part! In retrospect, the aspect I most underestimated was the need for a singular focus while in the midst of a sea of distractions from naysayers on one hand and supporters with extraneous ideas on the other. In these modern times, it isn't about being everything to everybody. Rather, success comes from solving a very specific problem for a niche group of customers.

The poem by Robert Frost could apply to any number of aspects in life, but it certainly appears to be right on target for entrepreneurs. For our entire lives, people call us to the well-traveled paths, but there is more to be accomplished on the less-traveled paths.

Of all the ways to spend a career, that of an entrepreneur might be the most misunderstood. Countless new acquaintances have remarked to me, "I always wanted to start a business, but..." There is a magnificent difference between those who raise their hand to take charge of their own destiny and those who merely consider it. I salute anybody who hangs the proverbial shingle to take their shot at success at any scale. Those who say "I think I have a better way" or "I can do it better, or cheaper, or faster" are everyday heroes in the field of business.

In this chapter, we will explore what it means to be an entrepreneur, from a definition that includes more than business owners alone to the characteristics that separate great entrepreneurs from the masses.

WHAT MAKES AN ENTREPRENEUR

That of an entrepreneur is a special title that is earned, not bestowed. When you are one, you know it. If you have to claim it, you probably aren't. Americans enjoy the benefit of the freedom to make such choices for ourselves.

> *Being powerful is like being a lady. If you have to tell people you are, you aren't.*

—Margaret Thatcher

There are many perspectives on the definition of entrepreneurship. Some would limit the title to only those who start a business. Others, including myself, look deeper. For example, Ray Kroc was the mastermind who built the global McDonald's empire we know today. Ray didn't start McDonald's. But he was inspired to purchase a small, local hamburger chain for which he had a vision. He proceeded to build that business into his lofty vision that few others could see. *My definition of entrepreneurship relates more to adopting a vision, taking the risk and exercising the discipline and creativity to cultivate that vision into reality.*

In fact, I expand the definition even one step further to include not only traditional self-employed business owners but also a select breed of managers who aren't business owners at all. While I have been a business owner for nearly my entire adult life, I am comfortable with sharing the classification with innovation leaders within other organizations who take comparable risks to build a vision. Their risks are often as great, even if they take a different form.

Take the example of the Medical Records Director or manager of a transcription department within a healthcare facility. While most are not entrepreneurs, they could be. By finding a vision of an innovative future, becoming a champion advocate for that vision and demonstrating the conviction to see it through, that person can become more than a manager; that person can become a leader.

In 1988, as a junior in the mechanical engineering curriculum at Rose-Hulman, I was fortunate to land a job at a nearby plant of Bemis Company. Bemis was a Fortune 500 company with many divisions. This plant was the headquarters for the Film Division, which produced plastic film used primarily for packaging. At that time, the facility had nearly 500 employees and was in the midst of a series of significant expansions. (They would grow to more than 1,000 employees at this site alone over the following decade.) My position was part-time, as I could only manage to work about 30 hours per week while school was in session. To my benefit, there was no formal internship program at the time. My manager, an engineer and Rose-Hulman grad himself, treated me as a regular project engineer. In my first year, I executed projects totaling approximately $3 million of capital spending. This was a dream job for an aspiring young engineer, manager and entrepreneur. The following year, I accepted a generous job offer from the company to begin my full-time career there.

From this position, I witnessed the best and the worst of "big company" work, the corporate ladder and internal politics. I saw how bright, energetic people could become frustrated with the big business bureaucracy, but I also witnessed rare examples of "company" people who set aside their fear of failure and resisted the temptation to settle into a rut. Occasionally they endured defeat, but more often, they succeeded in spreading optimism and consolidating resources around their initiatives. These few people were entrepreneurs.

THE ROOTS OF ENTREPRENEURSHIP

The earliest human beings survived as hunters and gatherers. They lived, or died, based on the risks they took and what they accomplished in a given day. Later generations learned to farm. Through this seasonal method of production, their output soared and their daily risk declined, but there was still no safety net. A hard worker who took intelligent risks based on accurate assumptions fared much better than one who struggled with his work ethic or made marginal risk decisions. In other words, humanity began with entrepreneurship.

The agricultural economy eventually gave way to the Industrial Age. As farming had replaced hunting as a primary means of production, factories replaced the family farm. By the end of the 19th Century, only a declining fraction of the population was needed to produce enough food for the American economy. As productivity soared in farming, factories emerged as both a way to utilize available human labor and as a way to leverage that labor with innovative new machines. As farms had once allowed humanity to produce more than hunting did, now machinery allowed us to produce more than farming.

Late in the 20th Century, the Information Age emerged. The U.S. economy began to experience a decline in the number of industrial jobs and significant growth in the number of information-related jobs. An MT, of course, is an information worker. As the plow had replaced the bow and arrow and the factory had replaced most family farms, the computer network and related service-industry jobs have replaced many factories. Again, productivity expanded and overall standards of living increased.

As a consequence of these transitions, workers have become more specialized and largely insulated from daily accountability of success and failure, namely, profit and loss—so much so that entrepreneurship appears to most people to be an alternative lifestyle!

To the contrary, exercising our entrepreneurial spirit is built into our humanity. The comic strip Dilbert[1] by Scott Adams depicts a fictional character who has been demoralized by the mundane work environment wrapped up in the modern cubicle-defined office. The comic strip is very funny, but only because it taps into our universal understanding of a disconnect between most workers and a thorough sense of satisfaction. Philosophers have long noted that all people yearn for a sense of meaning in their lives. Even family and other personal relationships cannot fully satisfy this need. We spend so much time working in our careers that it is important to our sense of self to feel connected to a worthy purpose. The importance of a sense of vision follows.

RISING TO THE NEXT LEVEL

Whether a business owner or a manager, leaders must consider where they find themselves in their career today. Do they feel as if they have supreme control over their destiny, or do they feel a little like Dilbert? Most people feel somewhere in between, but there is always a next level. It takes a lot of courage to take the next step, but the rewards and self-fulfillment are worth the risk. Most of us feel limited, but something that separates the great entrepreneurs from the masses is their belief in their own vision and an attitude of *whatever it takes.*

Just as a person employed by others can carry and exercise the entrepreneurial spirit, some self-employed people can find themselves void of it. It isn't about where they are but where they are headed that matters most.

Even successful business owners and managers should take pause. A traditional transcription service company, for example, is a well-defined model. Someone could start and successfully operate such a business without having made the choice to take an innovative level of risk. The question becomes, "What will that person do when they realize continuing the status quo is suddenly the risky choice?" More importantly, will they step up to the next level when they recognize an opportunity to accomplish significantly more?

My message is that anybody can become an entrepreneur—regardless of their current standing. The only requirement is that they prepare to become a leader,

---

1.   The comic strip is available online at www.dilbert.com.

to take the road less traveled. By doing so, they earn the opportunity to accomplish dramatically more, to help others and to achieve the self-fulfilling success they deserve.

9

Scaling a Small Enterprise

People pretend not to like grapes when they are too high for them to reach.

—Marguerite of Navarre

Growing a small business presents challenges in all aspects of management. When we talk about scaling[1] a small business, we are specifically referring to the growth in the business's production capacity to serve more customers. We will examine other planes of growth in coming chapters.

In today's paradigm, business managers draw a close parallel between the capacity to produce reports and their workforce of transcriptionists. Scaling a company is a process of building infrastructure capacity through the strategic development of internal and external resources.

FRANCHISING

Small businesses generally take advantage of external resources out of necessity. They buy services and output from others that they could not afford to fully implement themselves. This is the root of franchising. When a new entrepreneur purchases a Subway or UPS Store franchise, he or she is essentially saying, "I want to be in business, and I want to limit my responsibilities to certain aspects of the business while others are performed for me."

This process gained popularity during the industrial period as entrepreneurs established local sales facilities for products manufactured in central factories. Automobile dealerships make a good example. Other arrangements evolved in which the prominent brand name was not that of the manufacturer—but rather that of the retailer. The InfraWare platform is a hybrid system that allows the transcription service organization to maintain their own prominent branding.

---

1. Scaling means to grow to a greater magnitude.

The website, for example, on which their customers can view the queue and reports can show the transcription company's name and logo as if it were their own.

OUTSOURCING

Larger enterprises go through cycles of expanded outsourcing and bringing functions back in-house. They apply a rational science to learning in a manner in which they can perform best and in which others can contribute to their mission most effectively.

THE NEED FOR A PARTNER

The depth of IT resources involved in adopting SRT for reliable day-to-day operations is outside the reach of all but the largest transcription service companies. The servers, development, licensing arrangements and data management tasks require skilled personnel and deep capital investments. Faced with that limitation, it is no wonder that most companies have ignored the technology. And like grapes out of reach, they will pretend not to like it. As others benefit from it, their dislike will be validated, as we all dislike the effects of market trends which are out of our favor.

So what should an entrepreneur do with knowledge of new technology? They can't just bite off a new chunk of technology as if they had deep enough resources to acquire, implement and maintain it properly. On the other hand, they can't simply ignore the technology just because they don't have the personnel or resources. That would be a plan for obsolescence. They need to succeed, and they can't afford to take a backseat to anyone. The answer is to engage a partner.

SELECTING A PARTNER

Choosing a partner to outsource a sensitive portion of the business is a weighty task. Often, it involves a balancing act between reliability and value. We often find that the most stable and dependable vendors are too costly to fit our value requirements. On the other hand, we find that the most attractive pricing often comes from vendors who might not be dependable in the long-term. Small businesses need resources that are *just right*.

Seek out a business partner who complements the business's strengths and needs.

10

Promoting Growth

Drive thy business, or it will drive thee.

—Benjamin Franklin

Recent chapters have focused on increasing capacity to produce lines and reports. Since demand for MT services exceeds supply, additional capacity is readily required. In fact, the demand for capacity, and the potential for it, is significant enough for dramatic growth, not just incremental growth. The entrepreneurial spirit would suggest taking full advantage of this opportunity.

This chapter focuses on developing promotional plans to drive sales for growing the business. As such, it applies more to owners and managers of transcription service companies than to managers of internal transcription service departments. As an alternative to those managers, please see the following Internet link for insightful considerations for promoting a different kind of growth for managers of internal departments.

---

①Internet Expansion
www.infraware.com/growbizbook/internal

The old adage "Build it, and they will come" is not a reliable proverb—especially in a service industry. Effectively promoting a firm's abilities is essential. Ben Franklin's 18th-century observation is still applicable today. We need to be proactive in driving our businesses.

Those who do their part to meet the overall demand for transcription services will simultaneously secure their own business's future.

SATISFACTION

Satisfaction is a function of *expectation*. There may be no other insight as valuable as this one for a service provider. Strong customer satisfaction is necessary to grow the business, and it follows that managing expectations is just as important as managing quality.

The need for quality is often obvious. In our industry, it takes the form of accuracy, turnaround time, etc. Expectations are sometimes overlooked, but that is the other side of the equation. For example, if a provider intends to return reports in 24 to 48 hours and they return several in a row to a physician in about 25 hours, they might feel as if they had performed at the top of their game. If, however, the physician's expectation were 24 hours, his perception would naturally be that the provider was consistently late. One reality; two very different perceptions.

PROTECT EXISTING BUSINESS

Insulation

Build incentives for customers to stay and barriers to changing away to other vendors. For example, if an MT has a contract with a customer for 16 cents per line, she could revise the contract to leave the rate at 16 cents at a level somewhat below their recent volume. Set higher rates for lower volume levels. This will help keep that customer from shifting work to another vendor.

Value-Added Pieces

Add value with low-or no-cost add-on services that make it hard for a customer to leave or that build confidence in their perception of the service. Give the regular contacts something to talk about in meetings (that makes them look good—yes, them). Show them reports, such as accuracy statistics or turnaround time.

COMMUNITY SERVICE ORGANIZATIONS

Join groups that will contain prospective customers or relationships with them. Service clubs such as Rotary and Kiwanis foster relationships that yield long-term benefits. Join local boards or board committees.

When people participate in such functions, they are generally in an optimistic mood. They feel good about themselves and good about the others who are laboring with them for a noble cause. Of course, nobody should join such a group and immediately begin marketing to them or expect a first-year return on the investment in time. To the contrary, they should enter such a role with humility and without expectation for personal gain. My point is that by doing so, they will begin to be seen as a community leader and opportunities will naturally present themselves.

People buy services, and people buy from people they know and like.

Rotary Experience

I am proud to be a Rotarian. In the mid-'90s, I was on the board of directors of our local Junior Achievement organization. When I became chairman of that board, the executive director asked me to consider joining Rotary. He suggested that it would be enriching for me and would provide exposure for my role in Junior Achievement. He was right; it has. The personally enriching component of being a Rotarian is so rewarding that it is difficult to describe. That is tangential to the subject but is something very real.

I had been in Rotary for just about a year when I was asked if I would present a program on the impact of the Internet on local businesses. This member of the programming committee was only vaguely familiar with my business, but he thought I might have an interesting story to tell. (Looking back, I realize I could have been more proactive by seeking out such an opportunity to speak. Clubs such as Rotary often have holes in their schedules and are relieved when someone offers to present on a week when they do not have an outside speaker.) The result of this experience was an important customer opportunity. Immediately after the presentation, the president of the club approached me and said that he was glad to learn what my company did. He was the Chief Operating Officer (COO) of one of the largest insurance sales organizations in our regional market. They were growing through acquisitions, and he was going to need help building their computer network to handle the additional load and to reach remote offices. We had a nice chat, and I followed up with a letter offering to meet with him to discuss our services. Some weeks later, in the salad line before a Rotary meeting, he asked me if I was familiar with a software brand that had been recommended to him. I was, and he suggested we meet to discuss their plans. What followed was a lucrative customer relationship. He became our largest client over several years. This example shows how becoming involved in a community organization can lead to lucrative customer relationships, but it also demonstrates that these opportunities will present themselves in a variety of unexpected ways. When working with influential business leaders, opportunities present themselves in their own time.

United Way Experience

After I had served as a volunteer in various roles within my community's United Way chapter for many years, I was eventually asked to join the board of directors. This happened to be the same year that I started InfraWare, a provider of automation services for transcription services for organizations. While we had been developing our application service provider model for many months, we had not yet sought out customers or even beta-test candidates. At one of my early United Way board meetings, I sat next to the CEO of our community's largest hospital. As people will do, he politely asked what was new. Stricken with the opportunity to tell someone in his position about my new venture, I briefly and enthusiastically told him what we were developing. He was intrigued and told me he thought it was something worth discussing with the medical records staff at the hospital.

I was careful not to overuse that experience by dropping his name frequently or involving him too often, but at critical times during the discussions at other levels in the organization, it was very helpful that those involved knew that "David was interested."

How to start? It's easy. Just show up. Call the local United Way, Volunteer Action Center or similar community agency. They will know where volunteers are needed. Go to events that are advertised. Wear a nametag (with company name) to board meetings. Overspend for a nice one.

Don't be concerned about how it begins. Help is always needed, and by showing enthusiasm, promotions to board committees and special events come easily in non-profit organizations. Introverts may not buy my assertions that it is *easy* to get started. I am a recovering introvert, so I understand completely. Believe me when I say that this is a non-competitive space that is eager to have help. Step out of your comfort zone to make a couple of calls and visits.

I, who so love a hermit life for a good part of the day, find myself living in public, and almost losing my identity.

—Elizabeth Blackwell

BE PROACTIVE

Some of my favorite books are those by best-selling author Stephen Covey[1]. His no-nonsense approach to adopting proven, effective habits that improve human performance is refreshing and powerful. The foundation of Covey's observations is that it is important to be *proactive*. Many understand this word to mean assertive or aggressive. While these can be true, it also involves a brief degree of reservation. When something significant happens in our world, we are often driven to an immediate emotional response. By studying the most effective people, Covey observed that they shared the capacity to set aside that emotional response in favor of a chosen response from their rational minds. Our brains generate the emotional response almost immediately, but a rational response takes a little time to generate. It's validation for the old adage "Count to ten before saying anything." In business, the *fight or flight* response is rarely appropriate. Since our lives aren't on the line, such a response is too dramatic and counterproductive.

When thinking of admirable public leaders, notice that they reserve their passion and emotion for those occasions when they are presenting their well-groomed messages. When they are attacked by challengers or face defeating circumstances, they appear reserved and collected. This allows them to present themselves in such a way that we see a very mature "big person." These habits are extremely useful in our business relationships with employees, vendors and customers.

Honor commitments, no matter how small. Returning phone calls is one of the most fundamental examples. Even when delivering unsubstantial or bad news, it is better to demonstrate a standup character than to avoid the interaction. After a phone call with negative subjects, you will feel better for having been reliable and honest, and the customer will, too.

---

1.   Stephen Covey is the author of the *Seven Habits of Highly Effective People* and many other books on the subject of applying reliable principles to human performance and leadership. If I were to suggest your next book, this would be it.

DO'S AND DON'TS

There is no one secret formula to successfully operating a business. Each organization has a unique set of competitive circumstances and opportunities. There are, however, a number of things to strive to achieve and others to avoid.

Personal actions

Be on time. Consistent with returning phone calls, be on time to appointments. Some businesspeople take this very seriously, and it is a very inexpensive way to earn their confidence.

Dress the part. When you are with clients and others in the business community, look professional. What you wear projects against your business. Dressing too expensively can lead customers to think, "I can't afford them." If you are shabbily dressed, they will think, "I don't trust them." Your objective should be to look clean and fresh, not stiff.

Make eye contact. When you are with business contacts, make eye contact to show them sincerity.

Business strategy

Find a niche. One of the mistakes many small business leaders make is to try to be all things to all people. Modern business is more about serving niche markets. Eventually, you will find a sweet spot, a type of customer that you can serve more effectively than your competitors can. As that happens, you can capture and recite success stories as part of your marketing plan.

Consider an SLA. A Service Level Agreement can be a simple document that outlines the performance terms of your service to your customers. It is a guarantee of sorts. It spells out commitments and consequences (such as turnaround time and accuracy). An SLA can be very useful for marketing your service.

Avoid frequent billing credits. When you fail your customers (and we all do so from time to time) you should be quick to accept responsibility. However, I suggest avoiding frequent billing credits for big complainers. Responding to these can just validate their complaining and ensure more of the same. Instead, set expectations that both of you can accept.

PRODUCE A FLYER TO MARKET THE BUSINESS

Keep it simple. Don't overreach with fancy graphics, folds or elements you can't afford to master. It is better to produce a professional-looking piece that is on the simple side than to venture into elements that look unfinished. Go as far as is professional—even if it is just text.

Tailor your message. Most small-business people try to say too much. Realize how little time the flier will get from most readers (less than 3 seconds) by tailoring the message to be clear and concise.

Have someone proofread it. Even professionals in the fields of writing and communication can suffer from a weakness in proofing their own work. This document is critical. Imagine the impression on a customer who reads a promo and sees an error.

Drop off your flyer at medical offices and prospective customer locations. While mail is cheaper (and tempting), it is less likely to be effective. Most professionals will toss out promotional (a.k.a. junk) mail without opening it. Showing up in person allows for the opportunity to make a positive impression on at least one person. So dress up, and make some rounds. Smile and introduce yourself and your business.

ⓘInternet Expansion
www.infraware.com/growbizbook/promocalendar

11

Coping with Growth

One machine can do the work of fifty ordinary men. No machine can do the work of one extraordinary man.

—Elbert Hubbard

Managing a growing business is a challenging endeavor. It can test our personal limits in ways we never imagined. With the right preparation, it can be the most rewarding experience of your career. Without the right tools, well, even success can be brutal; failure, unspeakable.

In this chapter, we will examine some fundamental business lessons that not only can make the difference between success and failure, but the difference between enjoying the success or not. Effective implementation of information technology is a cornerstone of managing growth, but this chapter deals primarily with other aspects of management.

NOT ENOUGH TIME

One of the most common complaints I hear from business owners and managers is that they simply don't have enough time to run their businesses the way they would like. In fact, as you read my suggestions for driving growth, you might have asked yourself, "How could I possibly find the time to get out to the field to sell my services *plus* join a service club, nonprofit board and attend other community events? I barely keep a handle on my business now."

To that question, I can only answer, "I understand." It is wrong, to think you can't afford the time, but I understand. I understand, because I have been there. While exploring abstract thoughts such as these, it is sometimes helpful to take them to their natural limits. For example, does the president of the largest transcription company in your state have enough time to do it right? What about the President of the United States? Of course they do. It is a matter of effectiveness.

The most effective people are skilled at choosing what to work on, what to delegate and what to simply ignore.

Some entrepreneurs find it difficult to delegate. The saying goes, "If you want it done right, do it yourself." To the contrary, I'd suggest, "…give it to someone you trust."

As you manage human resources (direct employees, or subcontractors) think of personnel as either producers or staff. Producers are those who earn revenue for the company. They *do* what the company *does*. In your business, these are primarily transcriptionists today. A strong argument can be made that sales work is also production. Management, customer service, billing and other activities are all very important, but they are not production. We will consider those done by staff.

Manage your producers and staff differently. In a small business, nearly everyone needs to wear many hats, but you should structure your business so producers have simple, clearly defined goals. Remember, "What gets measured, gets done." So eliminate obstacles and reward production. Staff, even yourself when performing staff functions, should be aligned to support producers and handle the routine business events that make selling, producing and delivering your service more convenient for customers and producers.

If you are an entrepreneur who is aspiring to grow a business, your primary role is unique in your company. While you will help with nearly everything, your most important role is neither that of staff nor producer. As a leader, your role is to create the environment in which producers and staff can succeed. By exercising leadership, you foster a business atmosphere that can be scaled to a larger size by using additional qualified people.

FINANCIAL MANAGEMENT

Another concern to owners of growth companies is cash management. As sales grow, we make additional investments in capital equipment, in marketing and in accounts receivable. In fact, many businesses that fail actually do so while making a profit. How is that possible? It is really very simple. If your business's net profit is $5,000 per month but you are expanding at such a rate that you are investing $4,000 per month to grow the infrastructure and accounts receivable (AR) is growing by $3,000 per month, there is a $2,000 deficit. (To make matters worse, you might even have a tax liability in the neighborhood of $1,000, which expands that cash deficit to around $3,000 per month.) A continuous year of such profitable growth can burn through $36,000 in cash. Unless you have a solid financial plan for replenishing that cash, you can find yourself in a bind. Plans for marketing and other non-production expenditures could be put on hold, not because they aren't strategically correct investments, but because the resources aren't on hand to execute them.

Worse, some business owners don't manage cash closely, and if they are new to this concept, they can be caught off guard—too late. What you can do? Though not an exhaustive list, here are a few fundamental suggestions:

> Manage AR effectively. While there are many strategies for management of accounts receivable, I suggest that the most effective initiative can be to (politely) let your customers know that it is important to you. Remember that while receiving payment for services is very personal to a small-business owner, it is impersonal to those who approve invoices and process payments in large organizations.
>
> Think of your early experiences with a new customer as if they were training. These first impressions really stick. If you are passive about payment, they will remember. If you indicated it was important, they will remember.
>
> Consider an early payment discount. Some firms find success by offering a 1% discount for invoices paid within 10 days (early).
>
> Establish a credit line to cover most of AR. If you carry accounts receivable of $30,000, the commercial department of your local bank should be willing to open a credit line for you in the amount of $20,000 to $25,000. A credit line is easy to manage, and it provides your business with flexibility. When you don't need it, you simply leave the balance paid down to zero.
>
> Finance capital equipment. Even if you can afford to pay cash for new computers or other capital purchases you make, consider financing them. Doing so allows you to keep your cash for driving growth and maximum flexibility.

As a manager, you need options and flexibility. By conserving your own cash and using that of others when practical, you preserve options for the business. As this book is being written, interest rates are at historic lows. This advice might be tempered by different economic conditions, but the principle is that you can only borrow money when you don't desperately need it. By managing cash carefully even when the need isn't obvious, you protect yourself from "hitting the wall."[1]

---

1. Drawing on a marathon runner's analogy to running out of energy three-quarters of the way through a race, business owners commonly use this term to refer to running out of cash, causing a business failure.

Don't fear a little debt. When used properly, it is a powerful tool. In contrast to relying too heavily on consumer credit, commercial borrowing can help you acquire the resources you need to execute a successful business strategy.

STAFFING

Staffing your organization with the best team members is critical. The question is, how do you define "best," and can you afford the best?

In my own businesses, I have often struggled with those questions. We all worry about over-committing our cash flow by hiring people we might not be able to afford in the long haul. To be sure, such decisions must be made carefully and incrementally. There is risk involved in staffing well, but the risk isn't associated with the decision to do so. Rather, the risk is in choosing the right people. If the right people come onboard and your business model is sound, they will strengthen your financial position.

In addition to the fundamental knowledge of the particular area of the job (i.e., accounting, customer service, etc.), here are some things to observe:

Insist on a cover letter with résumé. The need for a résumé is obvious, but I have found that I can tell much more about a person's communication skills from a letter. The content can show the applicant's attitudes, communications skills and more.

Look for optimists. When you interview candidates and observe their personalities, look for optimists. Naysayers are more difficult to lead, and their pessimism is contagious to the rest of your team. Likewise, optimism is contagious. People with positive outlooks don't cost more, but your business and your customers get more.

Sell your business. In the interview process, while you are learning about candidates, share information about your company and accomplishments that would make them want to work with you. When they leave a first interview, you want them to tell their best friend, "XYZ Company is really neat. I hope to get an offer from them because it would be exciting to be a part of what they do." (You might have to remind yourself of the true importance of the work you produce. Set aside your knowledge of the day-to-day problems and frustrations. All businesses have those, and when the best applicant is sitting across from you, you are selling the job.)

Job descriptions are important, but so is flexibility. As a best practice, you need a written job description to start a search and to train new a new employee, BUT one benefit of a small business is that you can change your job design during the search/selection process based on personalities or skill sets that you find. There are many ways to organize a company or department. Over the years, some of the best people I have found have been during interviews for a position that wasn't an ideal fit for them. If at all possible, I make room for those people in the organization. Responsibilities can be shifted and realigned. The best people are worth such efforts.

Self-motivation is key. It is easy to say, and nearly every resumé says it, but that is something hard to fake. If you ask a candidate for examples from their career in which they demonstrated such motivation, you will learn a lot. Don't just listen to what they say. Read between the lines and trust your intuition. You can't just advertise for "self-motivated" and get it. You must be observant and selective.

REGENERATION

Eventually, you should make time for yourself, your family and your hobbies. I know the 60-hour work week as well as most business owners do. They are often necessary to get a business off the ground or through a growth phase. When the opportunity presents itself to delegate more and work more reasonable hours, it is important to exercise that option.

In addition to remembering the most important things in our lives, we can take comfort in knowing that it is actually best for our businesses that we regenerate. Time away from work is therapeutic, and it actually helps us gain perspective and work more effectively.

Money is better than poverty, if only for financial reasons.

—Woody Allen

CONCLUSION

The transcription service industry is poised for dramatic change in the immediate future. Those who ignore the signs are doomed to the same destiny as countless other business owners in other industries that evolved at the expense of established small businesses. While the number of service companies is likely to decline during this transition, those who adapt early can thrive in the new market conditions.

By embracing technology soon, you can grow your business as well as your margins. In addition to much greater profits, you can position your business for strategic survival. InfraWare offers the technology. Our platform is an easily adopted, low-cost, low-risk way to transform your business for the next generation of success. Of course, other vendors offer competing ideas, and you should consider the best fit for your organization.

Please challenge yourself to tap your entrepreneurial spirit by charging boldly into this new era. Best wishes for continued prosperity in your enterprise. If my team can be of assistance, please call on us.

Appendix

Margin Opportunity Worksheet

Compute the value opportunity using your own information. A sample can be found in Chapter 6.

Description	Rev(Cost)
Current	
Billing rate to end-user (price)	
Wholesale rate paid to sub (cost)	-
Difference (margin)	=
Assume 2-fold productivity increase	
Billing rate to end-user (price)	
InfraWare pre-processing cost	-
Wholesale rate paid to sub (cost) [divide current by 2]	-
Difference (new margin)	=
Assume 2.5-fold productivity increase	
Billing rate to end-user (price)	
InfraWare pre-processing cost	-
Wholesale rate paid to sub (cost) [divide current by 2.5]	-
Difference (new margin)	=
Assume 3-fold productivity increase	
Billing rate to end-user (price)	
InfraWare pre-processing cost	-
Wholesale rate paid to sub (cost) [divide current by 3]	-
Difference (new margin)	=

Glossary of Acronyms

AR—Accounts Receivable

ASP—Application Service Provider; also used for Active Server Pages by computer programmers

CEO—Chief Executive Officer

COO—Chief Operating Officer

CS—refers to CS Technology Center

DSL—Digital Subscriber Line

EMR—Electronic Medical Records

HIPAA—Health Information Portability and Accountability Act

HL7—Health Level Seven (standards body and associated messaging protocols)

HMM—Hidden Markov Modeling ISP—Internet Service Provider

ISP—Internet Service Provider

IT—Information Technology

LAN—Local Area Network

MBA—Master in Business Administration

MT—Medical Transcription, Medical Transcriptionist

MTI—Medical Transcription Industry

PC—Personal Computer

ROI—Return On Investment

SaaS—Software as a Service

SLA—Service Level Agreement

SRT—Speech Recognition Technology

TSC—Transcription Service Company

WWW—World Wide Web

Continuous speech recognition—speech recognition technology that allows authors to speak at their normal pace without pausing between words.

0-595-34482-8

www.ingramcontent.com/pod-product-compliance
Lightning Source LLC
Chambersburg PA
CBHW021007180526
45163CB00005B/1927